Cocktails

PaRragon

Bath · New York · Singapore · Hong Kong · Cologne · Delhi · Melbourne

This edition published by Parragon in 2010

Parragon Publishing
Queen Street House
4 Queen Street
Bath BA1 1HE, UK

ISBN: 978-1-4075-9471-2
Printed in China

Internal design by Terry Jeavons & Company

Notes for the Reader
This book uses imperial, metric, and U.S. cup measurements. Follow the same units of measurement throughout; do not mix imperial and metric. All spoon measurements are level: teaspoons are assumed to be 5 ml, and tablespoons are assumed to be 15 ml. Unless otherwise stated, milk is assumed to be whole, eggs and individual vegetables, such as potatoes, are medium, and pepper is freshly ground black pepper.

The times given are an approximate guide only. Preparation times differ according to the techniques used by different people and the cooking times may also vary from those given as a result of the type of oven used. Optional ingredients, variations, or serving suggestions have not been included in the calculations.

Recipes using raw or very lightly cooked eggs should be avoided by infants, the elderly, pregnant women, convalescents, and anyone with a chronic condition. Pregnant and breast-feeding women are advised to avoid eating peanuts and peanut products. People with nut allergies should be aware that some of the prepared ingredients used in the recipes in this book may contain nuts. Always check the packaging before use.

Picture acknowledgments
The publisher would like to thank Getty Images for permission to reproduce copyright material for the front cover

Cocktails

introduction

From the classic sophistication of a dry martini to the juicy delights of a fruit daiquiri and from the elegance of a julep to a colorful shooter, cocktails are as much a delight to the eyes as to the palate. They are flavorsome, fun, and designed to be shared—but as they are often potent, moderation is a useful word to keep in mind.

They are simply mixed drinks, usually based on one or more spirits or liqueurs and flavored with fruit juices, syrups, spices, and other mixers. (Nonalcoholic cocktails are generally based on fruit or vegetable juices.) Clearly, there is more to making a cocktail than simply tipping the contents of half a dozen bottles into a shaker.

Fortunately, hundreds of cocktails have been created and tested regularly since the first great cocktail era of the 1920s and new recipes are being devised all the time.

Cocktails may be shaken or stirred—the former are cloudy

because they contain egg white, cream, or fruit juices, while the latter are clear. A cocktail shaker is not essential but makes mixing easier and you feel more professional. Pour the ingredients into the shaker over

cracked ice, fit the lid, shake vigorously until the outside of the shaker is lightly frosted, then pour through a strainer (usually incorporated in the shaker) into glasses. However, make sure that you never add fizzy mixers, such as tonic water, to the shaker. If they form part of the cocktail, finish off with them once the drink has been poured. You can also use a blender and this is sometimes specified in the recipes for certain cocktails. Stirred cocktails are made by pouring the ingredients over cracked ice into a mixing glass—

basically a translucent glass pitcher—and stirred with a long-handled spoon before being strained into appropriate serving glasses. You can also use the goblet part of a cocktail shaker.

vodka & gin

Vodka, distilled from grain and filtered through charcoal, has long been a popular base for cocktails because it is a neutral spirit and virtually flavorless. This means that it mixes well with any number of liqueurs and nonalcoholic mixers, adding weight to the cocktail without affecting the flavor. Consequently, there are not only numerous classics based on vodka, but it is also often the spirit of choice for contemporary concoctions.

Recently, flavored vodkas—lemon, pepper, peach, cinnamon, chocolate, chili, and many others—have become fashionable. Although these are most often served straight, they have introduced a new dimension to cocktails. Adventurous would-be bartenders might like to try substituting one of these for standard vodka. Choose one that complements the main flavor of the drink.

Gin is also distilled from grain but it is then steeped with "botanicals," including juniper, which gives it both its name and characteristic flavor. It is the base of many famous cocktails, the most celebrated of which must be the Martini. It is a popular choice for the classic cocktail served in a small V-shaped glass because it works well with other spirits, liqueurs, and alcoholic drinks, but it is also frequently used as the base for longer, thirst-quenching coolers.

cosmopolitan

ingredients

SERVES 1

2 measures vodka

1 measure triple sec

1 measure fresh lime juice

1 measure cranberry juice

ice

twist of orange peel, to decorate

method

1 Shake all the liquid ingredients over ice until well frosted.

2 Strain into a chilled cocktail glass.

3 Dress with the twist of orange peel.

metropolitan

ingredients

SERVES 1

1 lemon wedge
1 tbsp superfine sugar
cracked ice
$^1/_2$ measure vodka
$^1/_2$ measure framboise
$^1/_2$ measure cranberry juice
$^1/_2$ measure orange juice

method

1 Rub the rim of a cocktail glass with the lemon wedge and dip into the sugar.

2 Put the cracked ice into a shaker and pour in the liquid ingredients.

3 Cover and shake for 10–20 seconds, until the outside of the shaker is misted.

4 Strain into the glass.

vodkatini

ingredients

SERVES 1

1 measure vodka

ice

dash dry vermouth

twist of lime peel, to decorate

method

1 Pour the vodka over a handful of ice in a mixing glass.

2 Add the vermouth, stir well, and strain into a cocktail glass.

3 Dress with the twist of lime peel.

the legend martini

ingredients

SERVES 1

2 measures iced vodka

1 measure blackberry liqueur

1 measure fresh lime juice

dash sugar syrup

method

1 Shake all the ingredients together until really well frosted.

2 Strain into an iced martini glass.

the modern martini

ingredients

SERVES 1

1 very ripe pomegranate

2 measures vodka

ice

method

1 Spoon the flesh of the pomegranate into a shaker and lightly crush or muddle.

2 Add the vodka and ice and shake well.

3 Strain into an iced martini glass.

bloody mary

ingredients

SERVES 1

dash Worcestershire sauce

dash Tabasco sauce

cracked ice

2 measures vodka

splash dry sherry

6 measures tomato juice

juice $1/2$ lemon

pinch celery salt

pinch cayenne pepper

celery stalk with leaves, and a slice of lemon, to decorate

method

1 Dash the Worcestershire sauce and Tabasco sauce over cracked ice in a shaker and add the vodka, splash of dry sherry, tomato juice, and lemon juice.

2 Shake vigorously until frosted.

3 Strain into a tall, chilled glass, add a pinch of celery salt and a pinch of cayenne pepper and decorate with the celery stalk and a slice of lemon.

long island iced tea

ingredients

SERVES 1

2 measures vodka

1 measure gin

1 measure white tequila

1 measure white rum

$1/2$ measure white crème de menthe

2 measures lemon juice

1 tsp sugar syrup

cracked ice

cola

wedge of lime, to decorate

method

1 Shake the vodka, gin, tequila, rum, crème de menthe, lemon juice, and sugar syrup vigorously over cracked ice until well frosted.

2 Strain into an ice-filled tall glass and top up with cola.

3 Dress with the lime wedge.

sex on the beach

ingredients

SERVES 1

1 measure peach schnapps

1 measure vodka

2 measures fresh orange juice

3 measures cranberry and peach juice

crushed ice

dash lemon juice

piece of orange peel, to decorate

method

1 Shake the peach schnapps, vodka, orange juice, and cranberry and peach juice over ice until well frosted.

2 Strain into a glass filled with crushed ice and squeeze on the lemon juice.

3 Dress with the orange peel.

moscow mule

ingredients

SERVES 1

2 measures vodka
1 measure lime juice
cracked ice
ginger beer
slice of lime, to decorate

method

1 Shake the vodka and lime juice vigorously over cracked ice until well frosted.

2 Fill a chilled, tall glass halfway with cracked ice cubes and strain the cocktail over them. Fill up with ginger beer.

3 Dress with the slice of lime.

screwdriver

ingredients

SERVES 1

cracked ice
2 measures vodka
orange juice
slice of orange, to decorate

method

1 Fill a chilled glass with cracked ice. Pour the vodka over the ice and top up with orange juice.

2 Stir well to mix and dress with the slice of orange.

black russian

ingredients

SERVES 1

2 measures vodka

1 measure coffee liqueur

cracked ice

method

1 Pour the vodka and coffee liqueur over cracked ice in a small, chilled glass.

2 Stir to mix.

kamikaze

ingredients

SERVES 1

1 measure vodka

1 measure triple sec

$^1/_2$ measure fresh lime juice

$^1/_2$ measure fresh lemon juice

ice

dry white wine, chilled

slices of cucumber and lime, to decorate

method

1 Shake the vodka, triple sec, lime juice, and lemon juice together over ice until well frosted.

2 Strain into a chilled glass and top up with wine.

3 Dress with the slices of cucumber and lime.

harvey wallbanger

ingredients

SERVES 1

ice

3 measures vodka

8 measures orange juice

2 tsp Galliano

cherry and slice of orange, to decorate

method

1 Fill a tall glass halfway with ice, pour the vodka and orange juice over the ice, and float Galliano on top.

2 Dress with the cherry and the slice of orange.

singapore sling

ingredients

SERVES 1

2 measures gin

1 measure cherry brandy

1 measure lemon juice

1 tsp grenadine

cracked ice

club soda

lime peel and cocktail cherries, to decorate

method

1 Shake the gin, cherry brandy, lemon juice, and grenadine vigorously over cracked ice until well frosted.

2 Fill a chilled glass halfway with cracked ice and strain in the cocktail.

3 Fill up with club soda and dress with the lime peel and cocktail cherries.

slow comfortable screw

ingredients

SERVES 1

2 measures sloe gin

orange juice

cracked ice

slice of orange, to decorate

method

1 Shake the sloe gin and orange juice over cracked ice until well frosted and pour into a chilled glass.

2 Dress with the slice of orange.

martini

ingredients

SERVES 1

3 measures gin
1 tsp dry vermouth, or to taste
cracked ice
green cocktail olive, to decorate

method

1 Pour the gin and vermouth over cracked ice in a mixing glass and stir well to mix.

2 Strain into a chilled cocktail glass and dress with the cocktail olive.

oasis

ingredients

SERVES 1

1 measure blue curaçao

2 measures gin

club soda

ice

wedges of lemon, to decorate

method

1 Shake all the liquid ingredients over ice until well frosted.

2 Strain into a chilled cocktail glass.

3 Dress with the wedges of lemon.

moonlight

ingredients

SERVES 4

3 measures grapefruit juice

4 measures gin

1 measure Kirsch

4 measures white wine

$^1/_2$ tsp lemon zest

ice

method

1 Shake all the ingredients together over ice and strain into chilled glasses.

mississippi mule

ingredients

SERVES 1

2 measures gin
$1/2$ measure crème de cassis
$1/2$ measure lemon juice
ice
crushed ice

method

1 Shake the ingredients vigorously over ice until well frosted.

2 Strain over crushed ice into a small chilled tumbler.

dry martini

ingredients

SERVES 1

1 measure London Dry gin
dash dry vermouth
ice
olive, to decorate

method

1 Shake the gin and vermouth over ice until well frosted and combined.

2 Strain into a chilled glass.

3 Dress with the olive.

road runner

ingredients

SERVES 1

2 measures gin

$1/2$ measure dry vermouth

$1/2$ measure Pernod

1 tsp grenadine

cracked ice

method

1 Shake the gin, vermouth, Pernod, and grenadine vigorously over cracked ice until well frosted.

2 Strain into a chilled glass.

tom collins

ingredients

SERVES 1

3 measures gin
2 measures lemon juice
1/2 measure sugar syrup
cracked ice
soda water
slice of lemon, to decorate

method

1 Shake the gin, lemon juice, and sugar syrup vigorously over cracked ice until well frosted.

2 Strain into a chilled tumbler and top up with soda water.

3 Dress with the slice of lemon.

white lady

ingredients

SERVES 1

2 measures gin
1 measure Triple Sec
1 measure lemon juice
cracked ice

method

1 Shake the gin, Triple Sec, and lemon juice vigorously over cracked ice until well frosted.

2 Strain into a chilled cocktail glass.

my fair lady

ingredients

SERVES 1

1 measure gin

$^1/_2$ measure lemon juice

$^1/_2$ measure orange juice

$^1/_2$ measure fraise

1 egg white

ice

method

1 Shake all the ingredients well over ice and strain into a cocktail glass.

tequila & rum

Distilled from the fermented, steam-cooked heart of the cactus-like *Agave tequilana*, the Mexican spirit tequila is a relative newcomer to the cocktail menu. It may have been a late starter but it has certainly made up for lost time and tequila-based cocktails are now among the most popular. The pale-colored Margarita, served in a salt-rimmed glass with a slice of lime, is an instantly recognizable cocktail icon. There are two types of tequila. Silver tequila is aged only briefly, usually in stainless steel vats. It is colorless and a little rough on the throat. Golden tequila is aged for at least three years in oak vats. It is golden in color, mellow in flavor, and more expensive.

Rum, distilled from the fermented sap of sugar cane, comes in three distinctive types, making it a very versatile spirit as a base for cocktails. Light-bodied white rum, which is actually colorless and clear, is widely used in classic-style cocktails. It is aged for just one year. Golden rum is made in the same way as white rum but is aged for three years, resulting in a more mellow flavor and a golden color. Dark rum has a much more powerful flavor because it is aged for five or more years in wooden barrels. It is then blended and may be darkened with caramel. It is the best choice for punches.

margarita

ingredients

SERVES 1

lime wedge, plus an extra wedge to decorate
coarse salt
cracked ice
3 measures white tequila
1 measure triple sec
2 measures lime juice

method

1 Rub the rim of a chilled cocktail glass with the lime wedge and then dip in salt to frost.

2 Put the cracked ice into a cocktail shaker. Pour over the liquid ingredients. Shake vigorously until a frost forms.

3 Strain into the prepared glass and dress with the extra wedge of lime.

margarita shot

ingredients

SERVES 8

1/2 lime, cut into wedges

2 tbsp fine salt

1 packet lime gelatin

1 cup hot water

4 tbsp Cointreau

scant 1 cup tequila

method

1 Rub the rims of 8 shot glasses with the lime, then dip in the salt.

2 Place the gelatin in a large heatproof measuring cup. Add the hot water and stir until the gelatin has dissolved. Let cool, then stir in the Cointreau and tequila to make up to 2 cups.

3 Divide among the prepared glasses and chill until set.

tequila cocktail

ingredients

SERVES 1

cracked ice

1 measure tequila

3 strawberries

1 tbsp cranberry juice

$1/2$ measure light cream

2 grinds pepper

method

1 Put the cracked ice into a cocktail shaker with the liquid ingredients.

2 Shake vigorously until well frosted, add the pepper, then strain into a chilled cocktail glass.

tequila mockingbird

ingredients

SERVES 1

2 measures white tequila

1 measure white crème de menthe

1 measure fresh lime juice

cracked ice

method

1 Shake the tequila, crème de menthe, and lime juice vigorously over cracked ice until well frosted.

2 Strain into a chilled highball glass.

tequila sunrise

ingredients

SERVES 1

2 parts silver tequila

cracked ice

orange juice

1 measure grenadine

method

1 Pour the tequila over cracked ice in a chilled highball glass and top up with the orange juice. Stir well to mix.

2 Slowly pour in the grenadine.

tequila slammer

ingredients

SERVES 1

1 measure chilled white tequila

1 measure lemon juice

chilled sparkling wine

method

1 Put the tequila and lemon juice into a chilled glass. Fill up with sparkling wine.

2 Cover the glass with your hand and slam.

jack frost

ingredients

SERVES 1

3/4 measure blue curaçao, iced
powdered sugar
1 measure chilled tequila
2 measures chilled cream
crushed ice

method

1 Dip the rim of a medium-size cocktail glass in the curaçao, shake off any excess, and dip immediately in sugar. Set aside in a cold place to dry and set.

2 Shake the rest of the ingredients and the curaçao over crushed ice until well frosted.

3 Pour carefully into the glass.

mad dog

ingredients

SERVES 1

1 measure white tequila

1 measure crème de banane

1 measure white crème de cacao

$1/2$ measure lime juice

cracked ice

lime and banana slices and a cocktail cherry, to decorate

method

1 Shake the first four ingredients vigorously over cracked ice until well frosted.

2 Strain into a chilled cocktail glass and dress with the lime slice, banana slice, and cocktail cherry.

shady lady

ingredients

SERVES 1

3 measures tequila

1 measure apple brandy

1 measure cranberry juice

dash lime juice

ice

method

1 Shake the ingredients over ice until well frosted.

2 Strain into a chilled cocktail glass.

wild night out

ingredients

SERVES 1

3 measures white tequila

2 measures cranberry juice

1 measure lime juice

ice

cracked ice

club soda

method

1 Shake the first three ingredients vigorously over ice until well frosted.

2 Fill a chilled highball glass halfway with cracked ice and strain the cocktail over them. Add club soda to taste.

piña colada

ingredients

SERVES 1

crushed ice

2 measures white rum

1 measure dark rum

3 measures pineapple juice

2 measures coconut cream

pineapple wedges, to decorate

method

1 Mix the crushed ice in a blender with the white rum, dark rum, pineapple juice, and coconut cream until smooth.

2 Pour, without straining, into a tall, chilled glass and dress with the pineapple wedges.

casablanca

ingredients

SERVES 1

3 measures white rum

4 measures pineapple juice

2 measures coconut cream

crushed ice

wedge of pineapple, to decorate

method

1 Shake all the ingredients except the fruit together over crushed ice and strain into a large cocktail glass with more ice, if you want.

2 Dress with the wedge of pineapple.

black widow

ingredients

SERVES 1

$^2/_3$ measure dark rum

$^1/_3$ measure Southern Comfort

juice of $^1/_2$ lime

dash curaçao

ice

club soda

twist of lime peel, to decorate

method

1 Shake the rum, Southern Comfort, lime juice, and curaçao together well over ice and strain into a chilled tumbler.

2 Fill up with club soda to taste and dress with the twist of lime peel.

mellow mule

ingredients

SERVES 1

2 measures white rum

1 measure dark rum

1 measure golden rum

1 measure Falernum (wine-based ginger syrup)

1 measure lime juice

ice

ginger beer

pineapple wedges and preserved ginger, to decorate

method

1 Shake the first five ingredients vigorously over ice until well frosted.

2 Strain the mixture into a tall chilled tumbler.

3 Fill up with ginger beer and dress with the pineapple wedges and preserved ginger.

ocean breeze

ingredients

SERVES 1

1 measure white rum

1 measure amaretto

$^1/_2$ measure blue curaçao

$^1/_2$ measure pineapple juice

crushed ice

soda water

method

1 Shake the white rum, amaretto, blue curaçao, and pineapple juice together over crushed ice.

2 Pour into a tall glass and top up with soda water to taste.

plantation punch

ingredients

SERVES 1

2 measures dark rum
1 measure Southern Comfort
1 measure lemon juice
ice
1 tsp brown sugar
sparkling water
1 tsp ruby port

method

1 Shake the rum, Southern Comfort, and lemon juice vigorously over ice with the brown sugar until well frosted.

2 Strain into a tall, chilled glass and top up, almost to the rim, with sparkling water.

3 Float the port on top by pouring it gently over the back of a teaspoon.

peach daiquiri

ingredients

SERVES 1

2 measures white rum

1 measure lime juice

$1/2$ tsp sugar syrup

$1/2$ peach, peeled, pitted, and chopped

method

1 Blend the ingredients together until smooth, then pour, without straining, into a chilled tumbler.

shanghai

ingredients

SERVES 1

4 measures dark rum

1 measure pastis

3 measures lemon juice

2 dashes grenadine

cracked ice

lemon slice and maraschino cherry, to decorate

method

1 Shake all the ingredients together over cracked ice until well frosted.

2 Strain into a chilled glass and dress with the slice of lemon and the cherry.

hurricane

ingredients

SERVES 1

ice

4 measures dark rum

1 measure lemon juice

2 measures sweet fruit cocktail or juice (passion fruit and orange are the usual)

club soda

slices of orange and whole cherries, to decorate

method

1 Fill a tall cocktail glass or highball glass with ice. Shake the rum, lemon juice, and sweet fruit cocktail until well combined and pour into the chilled glass.

2 Fill up with club soda and dress with the orange slices and cherries.

rum cooler

ingredients

SERVES 1

2 ice cubes

juice of 1 lime

$1^1/_2$ measures rum

$1^1/_2$ measures pineapple juice

1 medium-ripe banana, cut into chunks

lime peel, to decorate

method

1 Blend all the ingredients in a blender for about 1 minute, or until smooth.

2 Pour into a chilled glass and finish with a twist of peel.

whiskey & brandy

Whiskey is not only the oldest known spirit, it also has a venerable pedigree in the cocktail bar, forming the basis of many famous, although uncomplicated drinks. There are several different types of whiskey with distinctive flavors. Bourbon, distilled from a fermented cereal mash containing at least 51 percent corn and aged for over six years, is the best-known American whiskey, so it is not surprising that it features in a number of classic cocktail recipes. Also American, as well as Canadian, rye whiskey is made from cereals containing at least 51 percent rye, while Canadian whiskey is made from a mixture of cereals that vary according to brand. Scotch whisky may be single malt or blended—the former, made from dried, fermented, and distilled barley is aged for over 10 years and is too fine and expensive for cocktails. However, blended whiskey, a mixture of grain spirits and malt whiskies, is used. Irish whiskey is similar but the barley is dried in a different way.

Unlike other spirits, brandy is distilled from fermented grape juice or wine. Some of the most celebrated cocktails are brandy-based but they are not very numerous, perhaps because of its very distinctive flavor. Fruit brandies, such as applejack, are also used in cocktails.

manhattan

ingredients

SERVES 1

dash angostura bitters
3 measures rye whiskey
1 measure sweet vermouth
cracked ice
cocktail cherry, to decorate

method

1 Shake the liquids over cracked ice in a mixing glass and mix well.

2 Strain into a chilled glass and decorate with the cherry.

mint julep

ingredients

SERVES 1

leaves from 1 fresh mint sprig, plus an extra sprig to decorate

1 tbsp sugar syrup

crushed ice

3 measures bourbon

method

1 Put the mint leaves and sugar syrup into a small, chilled glass and mash with a teaspoon. Add the crushed ice and shake before adding the bourbon.

2 Dress with the mint sprig.

whiskey sour

ingredients

SERVES 1

1 measure lemon or lime juice

2 measures blended whiskey

1 tsp powdered sugar or sugar syrup

ice

slice of lime and a maraschino cherry, to decorate

method

1 Shake the lemon juice, whiskey, and sugar well over ice and strain into a cocktail glass.

2 Dress with the slice of lime and the cherry.

godfather

ingredients

SERVES 1

cracked ice

2 measures Scotch whisky

1 measure amaretto

method

1 Fill a chilled highball glass with cracked ice.

2 Pour in the whisky and amaretto and stir to mix.

thai cocktail sling

ingredients

SERVES 1

2 tbsp whiskey

1 tbsp cherry brandy

1 tbsp orange-flavored liqueur

1 tbsp lime juice

1 tsp jaggery

dash Angostura bitters

crushed ice

2 ice cubes

$^1/_2$ cup pineapple juice

1 small pineapple wedge, to decorate

method

1 Shake the first six ingredients well over crushed ice until frosted.

2 Place the ice cubes in a large glass. Pour the cocktail over and top off with the pineapple juice.

3 Dress with the pineapple wedge.

brooklyn

ingredients

SERVES 1

1 measure rye whiskey

$^1/_2$ measure sweet vermouth

dash maraschino

dash Amer Picon or angostura bitters

ice

cocktail cherry, to decorate

method

1 Stir the first four ingredients in a mixing glass with ice to chill, then strain into a chilled cocktail glass.

2 Add the cherry to finish.

new yorker

ingredients

SERVES 1

2 measures Jack Daniels

$^1/_2$ measure fresh lime juice

$^1/_2$ measure grenadine

ice

twist of orange peel

method

1 Shake the first three ingredients over ice well until frosted.

2 Pour into a chilled cocktail glass and serve with the twist of orange peel.

commodore

ingredients

SERVES 1

4 measures rye whiskey

1 measure fresh lime juice

2 dashes orange bitters

sugar, to taste

ice

strip of lime peel

method

1 Shake all the ingredients except the lime peel together over ice until well frosted.

2 Strain into a small tumbler or cocktail glass and dress with the lime peel.

millionaire cocktail

ingredients

SERVES 1

^{2}/$_3$ measure bourbon

^{1}/$_3$ measure Cointreau

2 dashes grenadine

1 egg white

ice

method

1 Shake the ingredients over ice.

2 Strain into a cocktail glass.

white diamond frappé

ingredients

SERVES 1

$1/4$ measure peppermint schnapps

$1/4$ measure white crème de cacao

$1/4$ measure anise

$1/4$ measure lemon juice

crushed ice

method

1 Shake all the liquid ingredients over the crushed ice until frosted.

2 Strain into a chilled shot glass and add a small spoonful of crushed ice.

strawberry kiss

ingredients

SERVES 1

1 measure Jack Daniels
1 measure strawberry syrup
3 strawberries
crushed ice
light cream

method

1 Blend all the ingredients, except the cream, in a blender on slow speed for about 10 seconds.

2 Pour into a chilled fluted glass and gently float the cream on top.

brandy cocktail

ingredients

SERVES 1

cracked ice

dash angostura bitters

2 measures brandy

$1/2$ tsp sugar syrup

slice of lemon, to decorate

method

1 Put the cracked ice into a cocktail shaker with a dash of angostura bitters, the brandy, and sugar syrup.

2 Shake vigorously until well frosted, then strain into a chilled cocktail glass and dress with the slice of lemon.

sweet singapore sling

ingredients

SERVES 1

1 measure gin
2 measures cherry brandy
dash lemon juice
ice
cracked ice
club soda
cocktail cherry, to decorate

method

1 Shake the first three ingredients vigorously over ice until well frosted.

2 Fill a chilled tumbler halfway with cracked ice and strain in the cocktail.

3 Fill up with club soda and decorate with the cherry.

rolls-royce

ingredients

SERVES 1

2 measures brandy

2 measures orange juice

1 measure Triple Sec

ice

method

1 Shake the ingredients over ice until well frosted.

2 Strain into a chilled glass.

stars & stripes

ingredients

SERVES 1

$^3/_4$ measure chilled cherry brandy

$1^1/_2$ measures chilled single cream

$^3/_4$ measure chilled blue curaçao

method

1 Pour the cherry brandy into a chilled shot glass. With a steady hand, gently pour in the cream to make a second layer and, finally, gently pour in the curaçao.

country cousin collins

ingredients

SERVES 1

2 measures apple brandy

1 measure lemon juice

$^1/_2$ tsp sugar syrup

crushed ice

dash orange bitters

sparkling water

slices of lemon, to decorate

method

1 Blend the apple brandy, lemon juice, and sugar syrup with crushed ice and a dash of orange bitters at medium speed for 10 seconds.

2 Pour into a chilled tumbler and top up with sparkling water.

3 Stir gently and dress with the slices of lemon.

cherry kitch

ingredients

SERVES 1

1 measure cherry brandy

2 measures pineapple juice

$1/2$ measure Kirsch

1 egg white

crushed ice

frozen maraschino cherry, to decorate

method

1 Shake the cherry brandy, pineapple juice, Kirsch, and egg white well over crushed ice until frosted.

2 Pour into a chilled, tall, thin glass and top with the frozen maraschino cherry.

napoleon

ingredients

SERVES 1

1 measure Mandarine Napoléon
1 measure cherry brandy
ice
lemon-flavored soda pop

method

1 Pour the liqueurs into a highball glass filled with ice.

2 Stir gently and then gradually top up with the soda pop.

moonraker

ingredients

SERVES 1

cracked ice

dash Pernod

1 measure brandy

1 measure peach brandy

1 measure quinquina

method

1 Put the cracked ice into a mixing glass. Dash Pernod over the ice and pour in the brandy, peach brandy, and quinquina.

2 Stir well to mix, then strain into a chilled highball glass.

black magic

ingredients

SERVES 1

$1^1/_4$ measures cognac

$^1/_2$ measure chocolate liqueur

$^3/_4$ measure mandarin liqueur

ice

1 tbsp cream

chocolate flakes, to decorate

method

1 Stir all the ingredients except the cream over ice in a mixing glass.

2 Strain into a chilled cocktail glass and carefully float the cream on top.

3 Dress with the chocolate flakes.

all things bubbly

If cocktails turn any occasion into a party, those made with sparkling wine or, better still champagne, will transform it into a celebration. Champagne comes only from a limited region of France and the name is protected. It is a sparkling wine produced as a result of secondary fermentation in the bottle, a special technique developed in the Champagne region. Vintage wines are too fine and costly for cocktails and even non-vintage champagne is expensive. However, combining it with other ingredients, such as fruit juice, in a cocktail does make it go further and provides an opportunity to give your guests a special treat. After all, there is little more elegant and delightful than a champagne breakfast. Sparkling wines, which may be made by a number of different methods, are a more economical substitute, especially if you are entertaining a large number of guests. There are some extremely drinkable bottles available.

Be careful when opening champagne or other sparkling wines that have a wire cage fitted over the cork. Obviously, you should never shake the bottle unless you are a winning racing driver. The force behind the cork is very considerable, so make sure that you are not inadvertently pointing it toward someone's face. Also, do not let go of the cork once you have released the wire.

champagne cocktail

ingredients

SERVES 1

1 sugar cube
2 dashes angostura bitters
1 measure brandy
chilled champagne

method

1 Place the sugar cube with the bitters in the base of a chilled flute.

2 Pour on the brandy and top up slowly with champagne.

buck's fizz

ingredients

SERVES 1

2 measures chilled fresh orange juice

2 measures chilled champagne

method

1 Fill a chilled flute halfway with orange juice, then gently pour in the chilled champagne.

kir royale

ingredients

SERVES 1

few drops cassis, or to taste

$1/2$ measure brandy

chilled champagne

method

1 Put the cassis and brandy into the bottom of a flute.

2 Fill up with champagne.

bellini

ingredients

SERVES 1

1 measure fresh peach juice, made from lightly sweetened, peeled, and blended peaches

powdered sugar

3 measures chilled champagne

method

1 Dip the rim of a champagne flute into some peach juice and then into the sugar to create a sugar-frosted effect. Set aside to dry.

2 Pour the peach juice into the chilled flute. Carefully top up with champagne.

mimosa

ingredients

SERVES 1

1 passion fruit
$^1/_2$ measure orange curaçao
crushed ice
chilled champagne
slice of star fruit, to decorate

method

1 Scoop out the passion fruit flesh into a pitcher or shaker and shake with the curaçao and a little crushed ice until frosted.

2 Pour into the bottom of a champagne flute and top up with champagne.

3 Dress with the slice of star fruit.

chicago

ingredients

SERVES 1

egg white or lemon juice

powdered sugar

1 measure brandy

1 dash Cointreau

1 dash angostura bitters

ice

champagne

method

1 Frost the rim of a glass with the egg white and sugar.

2 Shake the remaining ingredients except the champagne together with ice until frosted.

3 Strain into the prepared glass and top up with champagne.

black velvet

ingredients

SERVES 1

chilled Guinness
chilled champagne

method

1 Pour both drinks in equal quantities carefully (because they may fizz up) into a long beer or highball glass.

serpentine

ingredients

SERVES 1

$1/2$ measure green crème de menthe

cracked ice

champagne, chilled

slices of lime, to decorate

method

1 Pour the crème de menthe into the bottom of a flute with ice.

2 Pour in the champage and decorate with the slices of lime.

royal julep

ingredients

SERVES 1

1 sugar lump
3 sprigs fresh mint, plus extra to decorate
1 measure Jack Daniels
chilled champagne

method

1 In a small glass, crush the sugar and mint together with a little of the whiskey. When the sugar has dissolved, strain it into a chilled flute with the rest of the whiskey, and top up with champagne.

2 Decorate with the mint sprigs.

long tall sally

ingredients

SERVES 1

$^1/_4$ measure brandy

$^1/_4$ measure dry vermouth

$^1/_4$ measure Galliano

$^1/_4$ measure mandarin liqueur

ice

champagne or sparkling wine

method

1 Stir the first four ingredients over ice and pour into a tall, chilled glass.

2 Top up with champagne.

james bond

ingredients

SERVES 1

1 sugar cube
2 dashes Angostura bitters
1 measure chilled vodka
chilled champagne

method

1 Moisten the sugar with the bitters and place in the bottom of a chilled flute.

2 Cover with the vodka and then top up with champagne.

le crystal

ingredients

SERVES 1

$1/2$ measure Poire William

1 dash orange curaçao

ice

champagne

slice of fresh pear, to decorate

method

1 Shake all the ingredients, except the champagne, over ice until really cold.

2 Pour into a flute and top up with the champagne.

3 Dress with the slice of pear.

midnight cocktail

ingredients

SERVES 1

1 measure raspberry vodka

1 measure fresh raspberry juice

1 measure orange juice

ice

chilled champagne

raspberries, to decorate

method

1 Shake the vodka, raspberry juice, and orange juice vigorously over ice until well frosted.

2 Strain into a chilled flute and top up with champagne.

3 Stir gently to mix and dress with raspberries.

grape expectations

ingredients
SERVES 1

5–6 red or black grapes
ice
splash of mandarin liqueur
chilled pink champagne

method

1 Save 2 grapes for the glass. Crush the others in a small bowl. Add the ice and the liqueur, stir well, and strain into a chilled champagne glass.

2 Fill up with champagne.

3 Halve the remaining grapes and add to the glass.

pick-me-up

ingredients

SERVES 1

ice

3 dashes Fernet Branca

3 dashes curaçao

1 measure brandy

chilled champagne

slice of lemon, to decorate

method

1 Place the ice in a wine glass to chill.

2 Stir in the other ingredients gradually and top up with the champagne.

3 Dress with the slice of lemon.

sparkling gold

ingredients

SERVES 1

1 measure golden rum

1/2 measure Cointreau

chilled champagne

method

1 Pour the rum and liqueur into a chilled flute and top up with champagne.

french 75

ingredients

SERVES 1

2 measures brandy
1 measure lemon juice
1 tbsp sugar syrup
cracked ice
chilled champagne
twist of lemon peel, to decorate

method

1 Shake the brandy, lemon juice, and sugar syrup vigorously over cracked ice until well frosted.

2 Strain into a chilled highball glass and top up with champagne.

3 Dress with the twist of peel.

caribbean champagne

ingredients

SERVES 1

$1/2$ measure white rum

$1/2$ measure crème de banane

chilled champagne

slices of banana, to decorate

method

1 Pour the rum and crème de banane into a chilled flute.

2 Top up with champagne.

3 Stir gently to mix and dress with the slices of banana.

velvet mule

ingredients

SERVES 1

1 measure cassis

1 measure black sambuca

2 measures ginger wine

ice

cola

club soda or sparkling white wine

method

1 Stir the first three ingredients over ice until well frosted.

2 Strain into a frosted flute and top up with equal quantities of cola and club soda.

disco dancer

ingredients

SERVES 1

1 measure crème de banane

1 measure rum

few drops Angostura bitters

ice

sparkling white wine

method

1 Shake the first three ingredients well over ice.

2 Pour into a glass and top up with sparkling wine to taste.

flirtini

ingredients

SERVES 1

1/4 slice fresh pineapple, chopped

1/2 measure chilled Cointreau

1/2 measure chilled vodka

1 measure chilled pineapple juice

chilled champagne or sparkling white wine

method

1 Put the pineapple and Cointreau into a mixing glass or pitcher and muddle with a spoon to crush the pineapple.

2 Add the vodka and pineapple juice and stir well, then strain into a glass.

3 Fill up with champagne.

pink sherbet royale

ingredients

SERVES 2

1^1/$_2$ cups sparkling white wine, really cold

2 measures cassis

1 measure brandy

1 scoop crushed ice

blackberries, to decorate

method

1 Blend half the wine in a blender with the rest of the ingredients until really frothy and frosted.

2 Slowly whisk in a little more wine and pour into tall, thin glasses.

3 Dress with blackberries.

raspberry lemonade

ingredients

SERVES 4

2 lemons

1 cup confectioners' sugar

4 oz/115 g fresh raspberries

few drops vanilla extract

crushed ice

ice cubes

iced sparkling water

sprigs of lemon balm, to decorate

method

1 Cut the ends off the lemons, scoop out and chop the flesh, and place in a blender with the sugar, raspberries, vanilla extract, and crushed ice. Blend for 2–3 minutes.

2 Strain into tall glasses and top up with ice cubes and water.

3 Dress with sprigs of lemon balm.

apple fizz

ingredients

SERVES 1

$1/2$ cup sparkling cider or apple juice

1 measure Calvados

juice of $1/2$ lemon

1 tbsp egg white

generous pinch sugar

ice

method

1 Shake the first five ingredients together over ice and pour immediately into a highball glass.

nonalcoholic

There are many reasons why some of your guests may not want to consume alcoholic drinks, particularly ones that can be as potent as some cocktails. They may be under age, driving, pregnant, on medication, dieting, focusing on a healthy lifestyle, concerned about over-indulgence in alcohol, or simply not like it. However, cocktails are fun and it seems very unfair if those who don't drink alcohol are unable to join in. Sometimes called "mocktails," these innocuous drinks are the answer—colorful concoctions with adult flavors that are mostly made in the same ways as their alcoholic cousins.

In fact, many of these recipes are "innocent" versions of well-known and classic cocktails, but they are more subtle than the simple omission of the alcoholic ingredients. Just leaving out the spirit base would make the drink thin and lifeless, while omitting alcoholic mixers would spoil the flavor. Clever substitutes and appropriate alternatives have been used to give these drinks the zing that is characteristic of cocktails.

Equally, some of these nonalcoholic adult drinks have been specially created without any reference to the traditional cocktail bar. Delicious combinations of fruit juices, vegetable juices, fresh berries, and sparkling mixers give them a unique flavor that is all their own.

shirley temple

ingredients

SERVES 1

2 measures lemon juice

$^1/_2$ measure grenadine

$^1/_2$ measure sugar syrup

ice

cracked ice

ginger ale

slice of orange and a cocktail cherry, to decorate

method

1 Shake the lemon juice, grenadine, and sugar syrup vigorously over ice until well frosted.

2 Strain into a small, chilled glass filled halfway with cracked ice. Fill up with ginger ale.

3 Dress with the orange slice and the cocktail cherry.

virgin mary

ingredients

SERVES 1

3 measures tomato juice

1 measure lemon juice

2 dashes Worcestershire sauce

1 dash Tabasco sauce

cracked ice

pinch celery salt

pepper

slice of lemon and celery stalk, to decorate

method

1 Shake the first four ingredients vigorously over ice and season with celery salt and pepper. Strain into an iced glass.

2 Dress with the slice of lemon and the celery stalk.

soft sangria

ingredients

SERVES 4

6 cups red grape juice

1 cup orange juice

3 measures cranberry juice

2 measures lemon juice

2 measures lime juice

4 measures sugar syrup

ice

slices of lime and orange, to decorate

method

1 Pour all the juices and the sugar syrup into a chilled punch bowl and stir well.

2 Add the ice and the lime and orange slices and serve in chilled glasses.

faux kir royale

ingredients

SERVES 1

cracked ice

1^1/$_2$ measures raspberry syrup

sparkling apple juice

method

1 Put the cracked ice into a mixing glass.

2 Stir well to mix, then strain into a wine glass.

3 Fill up with apple juice and stir.

baby bellini

ingredients

SERVES 6

2 measures peach juice

1 measure lemon juice

sparkling apple juice

method

1 Pour the peach juice and lemon juice into a chilled glass and stir well.

2 Fill up with sparkling apple juice and stir.

cool collins

ingredients

SERVES 6

6 fresh mint leaves

1 tsp confectioners' sugar

2 measures lemon juice

cracked ice

sparkling water

fresh mint sprigs and wedges of lemon, to decorate

method

1 Put the mint leaves into a tall, chilled tumbler and add the sugar and lemon juice. Crush the leaves with a spoon until the sugar has dissolved.

2 Fill the glass with cracked ice and top up with sparkling water.

3 Stir gently and dress with the mint sprigs and wedges of lemon.

mini colada

ingredients

SERVES 2

6 measures cold milk

4 measures pineapple nectar

3 measures coconut cream

crushed ice

ice cubes

cubes of pineapple and a cherry, to decorate

method

1 Shake all the ingredients except the fruit together over ice until well chilled.

2 Pour into long glasses with ice cubes, and dress with the pieces of pineapple and the cherry.

cranberry punch

ingredients

SERVES 10

2^1/$_2$ cups cranberry juice

2^1/$_2$ cups orange juice

^{2}/$_3$ cup water

^{1}/$_2$ tsp ground ginger

^{1}/$_4$ tsp cinnamon

^{1}/$_4$ tsp freshly grated nutmeg

ice cubes (if serving cold)

frozen cranberries and their leaves, to decorate

method

1 Put the cranberry juice, orange juice, water, ginger, cinnamon, and nutmeg into a saucepan and bring to a boil. Reduce the heat and simmer for 5 minutes.

2 Remove from the heat and pour into heatproof glasses.

3 Chill and add ice cubes if serving cold. Decorate with the frozen cranberries and their leaves.

strawberry colada

ingredients

SERVES 2

4 cups strawberries

$1/2$ cup coconut cream

$2^1/2$ cups chilled pineapple juice

method

1 Reserve 4 strawberries to decorate. Halve the remainder and place in a food processor or blender.

2 Add the coconut cream and pineapple juice and process until smooth, then pour into chilled glasses and dress with the reserved strawberries.

pear & raspberry delight

ingredients

SERVES 2

2 large ripe Anjou pears

scant 1 cup frozen raspberries

generous $^3/_4$ cup ice-cold water

honey, to taste

raspberries, to decorate

method

1 Peel the pears and cut into fourths, removing the cores. Put into a food processor or blender with the raspberries and water and process until smooth.

2 Taste and sweeten with honey if the raspberries are a little sharp.

3 Pour into glasses and decorate with the raspberries.

perky pineapple

ingredients

SERVES 4

cracked ice

2 bananas

1 cup pineapple juice, chilled

$1/2$ cup lime juice

slices of pineapple, to decorate

method

1 Put the cracked ice into a food processor or blender. Peel the bananas and slice directly into the food processor or blender. Add the pineapple and lime juice and process until smooth.

2 Pour into chilled glasses, decorate with the slices of pineapple, and serve.

ginger fizz

ingredients

SERVES 1

ginger ale
sprigs of fresh mint
cracked ice
raspberries and a mint sprig, to decorate

method

1 Put the ginger ale and several mint leaves into a food processor or blender and process.

2 Strain into a chilled highball glass two-thirds filled with cracked ice. Dress with the raspberries and the sprig of fresh mint.

long boat

ingredients

SERVES 1

ice

1 measure lime syrup

ginger beer

wedge of lime and a sprig of mint, to decorate

method

1 Fill a chilled and frosted highball or tall glass two-thirds full with ice and pour in the lime syrup.

2 Fill up with ginger beer and stir gently.

3 Dress with the wedge of fresh lime and the sprig of mint.

st. clements

ingredients

SERVES 2

cracked ice
2 measures orange juice
2 measures bitter lemon
slices of orange and slices of lemon, to decorate

method

1 Put the ice into a chilled tumbler. Pour in the orange juice and bitter lemon.

2 Stir gently and decorate with the slices of orange and slices of lemon.

salty puppy

ingredients

SERVES 6

sugar

coarse salt

wedge of lime

cracked ice

$1/2$ measure lime juice

grapefruit juice

method

1 Mix equal quantities of sugar and salt on a saucer. Rub the rim of a small, chilled tumbler with the lime and dip in the sugar-salt mixture to frost.

2 Fill the glass with cracked ice and pour the lime juice over.

3 Top up with grapefruit juice.

coconut islander

ingredients

SERVES 1

1 pineapple

4 measures pineapple juice

4 tbsp creamed coconut

4 measures milk

2 tbsp crushed pineapple

3 tbsp flaked coconut

ice

fresh cherry, to decorate

method

1 Cut the top off the pineapple and remove the flesh.

2 Process or blend all the ingredients in a food processor or blender with a little ice for 30–40 seconds. When smooth and frothy, pour into the shell and dress with the fresh cherry.

cranberry energizer

ingredients

SERVES 2

1 1/4 cups cranberry juice

scant 1/2 cup orange juice

3/4 cup fresh raspberries

1 tbsp lemon juice

slices of orange, to decorate

method

1 Pour the cranberry juice and orange juice into a food processor or blender and process gently until combined.

2 Add the raspberries and lemon juice and process until smooth.

3 Pour the mixture into glasses and dress with the slices of orange.

citrus fizz

ingredients

SERVES 1

2 measures fresh orange juice, chilled

confectioners' sugar

few drops Angostura bitters

squeeze lime juice

2–3 measures sparkling water, chilled

method

1 Rub the rim of a flute with orange juice and dip into the sugar.

2 Stir the rest of the juices together with the bitters and then pour into the glass.

3 Fill up with sparkling water to taste.

cocobelle

ingredients

SERVES 1

3 measures cold milk

1 measure coconut cream

2 scoops vanilla ice cream

3–4 ice cubes

dash grenadine

long-shred coconut, toasted, for sprinkling

method

1 Put the first four ingredients in a food processor or blender and process until slushy.

2 Chill a tall glass and gently dribble a few splashes of grenadine down the insides.

3 Pour in the slush slowly and sprinkle with toasted coconut.

italian soda

ingredients

SERVES 1

cracked ice

$1^1/_2$ measures hazelnut syrup

sparkling water

slice of lime, to decorate

method

1 Fill a chilled Collins glass with cracked ice.

2 Pour the hazelnut syrup over and top up with sparkling water.

3 Stir gently and dress with the slice of lime.

cherry orchard

ingredients

SERVES 1

1 measure apple juice

1 measure pear juice

2 measures cranberry juice

ice

pink lemonade or cherryade

fresh or candied cherries and a wedge of pineapple, to decorate

method

1 Mix the fruit juices together over ice in a chilled glass.

2 Fill up with lemonade to taste and dress with the cherries and pineapple.

cocoberry

ingredients

SERVES 1

$1/2$ cup raspberries

crushed ice

1 measure coconut cream

$2/3$ cup pineapple juice

wedge of pineapple and fresh raspberries, to decorate

method

1 Press the raspberries through a sieve with the back of a spoon and transfer the puree to a blender.

2 Add ice, the coconut cream, and pineapple juice. Blend until smooth, then pour the mixture, without straining, into a chilled tumbler.

3 Dress with pineapple and fresh raspberries.

grapefruit cooler

ingredients

SERVES 6

2 oz/55 g fresh mint leaves, plus mint sprigs to decorate

2 measures sugar syrup

2 cups grapefruit juice

4 measures lemon juice

cracked ice

sparkling mineral water

method

1 Muddle the fresh mint leaves in a small bowl with the sugar syrup. Set aside for at least 2 hours to steep, mashing again from time to time.

2 Strain into a pitcher and add the grapefruit juice and lemon juice. Cover with plastic wrap and chill for at least 2 hours, until required.

3 To serve, fill 6 chilled Collins glasses with cracked ice. Divide the cocktail among the glasses and top up with sparkling water.

4 Dress with fresh mint sprigs.

lemon fizz

ingredients

SERVES 1

2 fresh lemons

crushed ice

peel of $1/2$ lemon

1 tbsp sugar

iced lemon-flavored soda pop

method

1 Squeeze the fresh lemons and pour the juice into a chilled highball glass filled with crushed ice.

2 Add the piece of peel and sugar to taste and stir briefly.

3 Add the soda pop to taste.